Practice Problems for

CREATIVE PROBLEM SOLVING

Third Edition

Practice Problems for

CREATIVE PROBLEM SOLVING

Third Edition

Donald J. Treffinger

Routledge
Taylor & Francis Group

NEW YORK AND LONDON

First published in 2000 by Prufrock Press Inc.

Published in 2021 by Routledge
605 Third Avenue, New York, NY 10017
2 Park Square, Milton Park, Abingdon, Oxon OX14 4RN

Routledge is an imprint of the Taylor & Francis Group, an informa business

Copyright ©2000, Donald J. Treffinger

Cover and layout design by Libby Lindsey
Cover Image © Eyewire, Inc

ISBN: 9781882664641(pbk)

DOI: 10.4324/9781003237211

CONTENTS

CONTENTS—CONTINUED

FIGURES

ACKNOWLEDGEMENTS

The practice problems included were initially developed with support from the Mahwah, New Jersey Public Schools. Initial field tests were conducted with students from:

- Honeoye, New York Central Schools;
- Newark, New York Central Schools;
- Mahwah, New Jersey Public Schools; and
- Allendale, New Jersey Public Schools.

The author gratefully acknowledges the support and contributions of:

- Catherine Bennett, Mahwah;
- Chet Greenleaf, Allendale;
- Jenny Lloyd, Honeoye;
- Patricia McEwen;
- Yvonne Saner, Newark;
- Cindy Shepardson, Newark; and
- Margaret Tiedemann, Newark.

Section I:
Introduction

This book contains 50 practice problems that are intended as resources for teachers or trainers who wish to provide Creative Problem Solving opportunities for their students. These problems were designed to represent a variety of different tasks or challenges in an open-ended, invitational format that we describe informally as a "Messy Situation."

Many people think of a problem only as something that is wrong, troublesome, or a matter of concern. When asked how they can tell that they have a problem, they report feeling angry, frustrated, tense, upset, nervous, frightened, or stressed. Indeed, those kinds of situations can be problems for anyone. But, our definition of a problem is broader, and it can also be positive. A problem can be a great opportunity, an exciting challenge, a wonderful chance to do or make or share something that you've always wanted. For that reason, we often prefer to discuss a "task" (a job, project, or piece of work that needs attention), "opportunity," or a "challenge." The brief Messy Situations presented in this book are broad tasks for which a person or group needs and wants a better way to understand and define the problem, some new options or possibilities, and/or a plan for taking action. In our contemporary view of CPS (e.g., Treffinger, Isaksen, & Dorval, 2000), it is not always necessary to use all of the CPS components or stages. These Messy Situations are intentionally very broad or general, leaving plenty of room for the problem solvers to think about what kinds of thinking will be most important and helpful for what needs to be accomplished.

These Messy Situations, like many of life's everyday opportunities and challenges, take a variety of forms, sizes, and shapes. They might concern a variety of situations in which people find themselves day in and day out. Thus, some of the Messy Situations in this book are people tasks (that is, situations involving the interactions or relationships among people). Others are planning tasks (that is, concerning more effective ways of organizing or managing a situation), and yet others are product tasks (that is, challenges that call for designing, inventing, or producing a new product of some kind).

When you are working on a CPS practice problem, there might be many different outcomes. There are no fixed, predetermined "right" or correct responses for how the Messy Situations should be handled using CPS, or for what the end results or outcomes will be. They might differ every time you use them with a different group. Since they are practice problems, some of the most important outcomes of any group's work with them will focus on developing the students' skills or proficiency in applying CPS methods and tools and on fostering positive attitudes about problem solving, particularly confidence in being able to apply CPS effectively. Learning and practicing the CPS process and discovering how it can be used successfully are much more important outcomes than the actual "solution" or problem outcome that the group might reach. Therefore, it is important to be very flexible in dealing with the kinds of products and decisions that might actually result from the students' work on the problems. Be certain to focus on understanding and applying the CPS methods and tools.

Some of the Messy Situations challenge the group to devise, design, or produce a tangible product, or a series of products. These might involve (or lead to) individual, small group, or team projects. Such projects, and the products they yield, can enhance students' involvement and heighten the value of the learning experience. Depending on the time available, the group's interests, and the resources available, you may decide that it would be better in certain circumstances to call for a prototype of a possible product, or even for a design or plan for a product (without actually completing the project or product). Once again, keep in mind that CPS process skills—knowing and using CPS methods and tools—are the principal outcomes that are of consequence for practice problems. Accordingly, feel free to modify the constraints or challenges of any of the Messy Situations.

When we first developed these practice problems, we began with a particular focus on the needs and interests of students in the intermediate and middle grades (grades four through eight). However, since the original publication of the first edition of this book, the Messy Situations have been used—with many clever and original modifications—by teachers who work with students from the primary grades through the senior high level in schools, and with a number adults in training programs and workshops. The problems are presented alphabetically by title. We have not attempted to organize them by topic, grade level, or difficulty, since we have found that they can be used in many different ways by imaginative trainers or group leaders. It is unlikely that anyone will use all of the CPS Practice Problems with any one group. Instead, we attempted to create an extensive set of resources from which you can pick and choose according to your students' needs and interests.

Before presenting the practice problems themselves, this section will consider several basic issues and provide background and suggestions for the teacher or trainer.

Why "Practice Problems," Anyway?

For many years, educators and trainers have discussed whether it is better to work on contrived, teacher-presented problems or "real" problems when teaching students Creative Problem Solving (CPS). Since 1980, my colleagues and I have been working with a model for organizing instruction in creative learning and problem solving (Isaksen & Treffinger, 1991; Treffinger, 1980; Treffinger & Feldhusen, 1998; Treffinger, Isaksen, & Dorval, 1994; Treffinger, Isaksen, & Firestien, 1982). This model deals with the appropriate and necessary balance between experience and practice in and out of the content context. That is, we do not believe that effective instruction is a matter of "real versus contrived" activities, but a systematic approach that blends foundations, realistic tasks, and real problems. This model is illustrated in Figure 1.

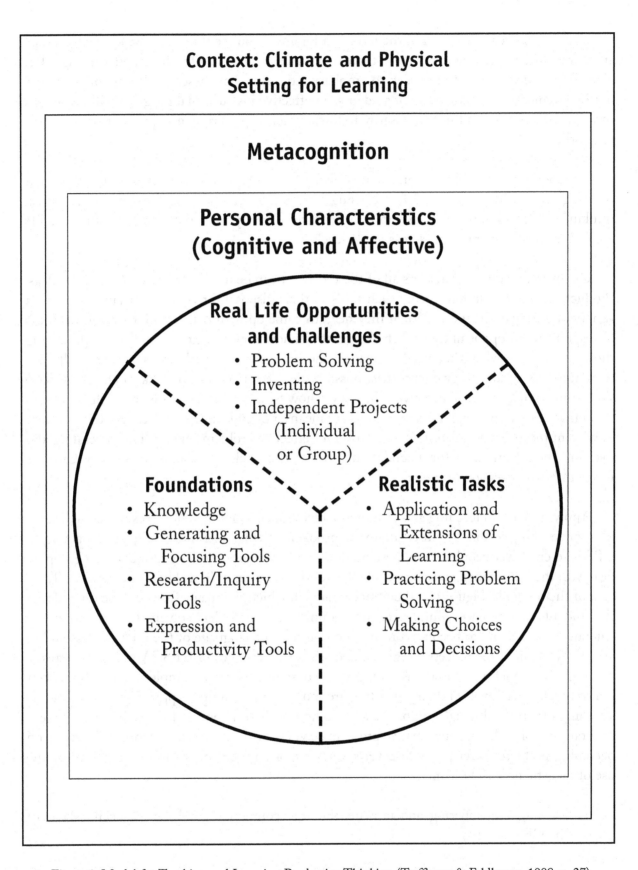

Figure 1: Model for Teaching and Learning Productive Thinking (Treffinger & Feldhusen, 1998, p. 27)

In the circle near the center of the model in Figure 1, you see three pie-shaped wedges, separated by dotted lines. These represent three major areas of focus for teaching and learning CPS. The circle and the dotted lines seek to emphasize the fact that these are flexible or fluid, and not hierarchical. With any group of students, an effective instructional program will involve all three areas, and they will not necessarily follow a strict or prescriptive sequence from one area to another.

The foundations involve learning and applying a number of tools for generating ideas—that is, using creative thinking—and for focusing ideas—that is, analyzing ideas or using critical thinking. These foundation skills can be introduced directly to the student, and then readily applied in most content areas, across grade levels.

Of course, no one ever masters all of the tools that can be used to generate or analyze ideas. Productive thinkers do have many such tools at their disposal for convenient application in a variety of everyday situations. When they need to come up with many, varied, or unusual ideas to respond to an opportunity or a challenge, they know how to help themselves in producing those ideas. And, when they need to analyze the strengths and weaknesses of several alternatives, improve an idea to give it the best possible chance for success, or make a choice or decision from among several alternatives, they know how to select and use tools that will help them to do that effectively, too. Foundation tools are means, not ends in themselves, but they are very important means in establishing a foundation for effective problem solving. The generating and focusing tools learned in the Foundations area of the circle are useful within any Creative Problem Solving session or group.

Applying CPS in teaching and training involves much more than doing exercises and activities, or teaching lessons about creativity or problem solving. The ultimate goal of training in CPS is to empower people to use these methods and strategies, working alone or in a group, to deal with the important situations and challenges they encounter in real life. The Realistic Tasks area of the model in Figure 1 is, therefore, an area in which the major focus will be on building the students' competence, confidence, and commitment as problem solvers. It is important for students to learn, and to become comfortable in using, the language of the CPS process and to apply any of the three process components or six specific stages of CPS. Working on realistic tasks involves much more than just doing an exercise or activity or completing a worksheet. It is also much more involved than just sitting around in a small group "popping" ideas for a brainstorming question, although (unfortunately) some people still confuse the use of a single idea-generating tool with applying creative problem solving. As people begin to work deliberately on becoming problem solvers, they discover several important goals that can be supported by the use of realistic tasks. These include:

- learning, remembering, and applying the three components and the six specific stages of the CPS process;

- recognizing opportunities to apply specific tools for generating or focusing options;

- dealing with the content of the task or problem itself;

- gaining an understanding of the important roles that people play in successful applications of CPS and learning the expectations associated with each role; and

- developing confidence in CPS and their own ability to be successful in applying it.

When people are familiar with a number of specific tools, they will naturally seek opportunities to apply them to challenging and complex tasks. They want to be problem solvers, not just participants in a set of exercises. As they learn and experience new methods, it can be very helpful to provide some experience with realistic practice problems in which the group can keep "one eye" on the problem and "the other eye" on the process tools they are learning to use. The most important outcomes when working in the Realistic Tasks area of the model are not the solutions to the problems themselves, but the students' competence in using CPS methods and tools and their confidence in their own ability to solve problems.

Realistic tasks must also be interesting or engaging, perceived by the students as relevant and worthwhile. Without interesting topics for motivational purposes, many students will simply fall away or lose motivation for CPS. Thus, for this collection, we attempted to create a diverse and varied set of resources so the problems might be seen as realistic, even though they are not strictly real problems for the pupils (since they are not problems for which the group began with a strong sense of ownership and involvement and a commitment to take action).

The third area of the circle in the model in Figure 1, Real Life Problems, represents an important eventual goal for any CPS instructional program: The students should be able to apply CPS methods and tools to the complex, open-ended, and ambiguous tasks and challenges they encounter in real life. We need to keep in mind that dealing with practice problems or the kinds of Messy Situations presented in this book is not the ultimate purpose or goal of instruction. To learn more about helping students apply CPS to real problems and challenges, building on and extending the experiences students will have with the activities in this book, you will find *The Real Problem Solving Handbook* (Treffinger, 2000b) to be a helpful resource.

Section II:
How to Use the CPS Practice Problems

In this book, the tasks or problems are presented as "Messy Situations," or challenges to be used as starting points for CPS. There are no predetermined correct solutions for any of the practice problems. Creating these Messy Situations involved seeking balance between two important concerns. On the one hand, the situation must provide enough information to enable a group to work on the problem productively. But, on the other hand, there must not be so much information, and the data must not be too specific, so the group will not be forced into a very limited, predetermined view of the situation or what needs to done. The practice problem must provide breadth, room for creativity, and imagination, but, at the same time, enough substance and structure to make the challenge workable for the group.

Feel free to use role-playing, socio-drama, or other small group methods to help students deal effectively with any of the Messy Situations. Feel free also to augment any of the Messy Situations with additional data to expand or fill in information to make the situation more relevant or interesting to the group. Use caution, however, when adding information to ensure that you do not inadvertently force a particular direction or solution onto the group as they work on the problem. Especially beware if there seems to be one, rather obvious way to interpret, define, or solve the problem. Our experience tells us that each group of students—whether young children, teens, or adults—will quite often surprise you by moving in very different directions than you might have assumed.

The CPS practice problems are not intended to be the participants' very first exposure to the CPS process stages or language. A number of resources might be helpful before you begin to work with any of these practice problems, to help students learn CPS terminology, to understand any of the specific CPS stages, or to practice using specific tools for generating or focusing options. One useful introductory resource for children is *CPS for Kids*, by Bob Stanish and Bob Eberle. For teenagers, Patricia Elwell's *CPS for Teens* would be very useful. For younger students, consider *Big Tools for Young Thinkers* by Susan Keller-Mathers and Kristin Puccio or *Adventures in Real Problem Solving* by Kristin Puccio, Susan Keller-Mathers, and Don Treffinger. For initial practice with CPS for children or teens, *Be a Problem Solver* by Bob Eberle and Bob Stanish is a useful resource. For adults, consult *Creative Problem Solving: An Introduction* (3rd ed.) by Don Treffinger, Scott Isaksen, and Brian Dorval or *Creative Approaches to Problem Solving* (2nd ed.) by Scott Isaksen, K. Brian Dorval, and Don Treffinger.

Any of the CPS practice problems in this book might serve as the basis for a working session of 45–60 minutes in length, although, with extensive role-playing and elaboration of the Messy Situations, many of them might easily be expanded for longer working periods or extended over several consecutive working sessions. The Messy Situations generally lend themselves most readily to CPS applications that begin with the Understanding the Problem component of CPS. However, keep in mind that effective CPS use does not always require using all three components of the model, nor using all six stages in a fixed or prescribed sequence.

Important Group Roles When Applying CPS

Four important roles are taken in any productive CPS application. These CPS practice problems will help you to acquaint groups with these roles and help them to practice any of the roles. The roles are:

- **Client.** The person who owns the problem and is responsible for taking action or following through on the decisions or outcomes. Although the CPS practice problems are contrived, in the sense that no one really "owns" any one of them, nor actually expects to carry out the solutions, appointing a group member to play the client role will be very helpful. It will enable group members to learn about the client's role and observe its importance in applying CPS. It will also help the focusing phase of any of the CPS stages to proceed smoothly.

- **Facilitator.** The teacher or trainer will usually serve as the group facilitator, although he or she may share this role with other participants in groups with prior CPS training and experience. The facilitator serves as the CPS process manager during the session.

- **Resource Group.** All of the other members of the group are called resource group members. Their role is to participate actively in generating ideas in any of the six CPS stages and to assist and support the client in the focusing phases. The resource group serves as the "think tank," helping the client produce more ideas—and more varied and unusual ideas—than he or she would have been able to think of alone.

- **Process Buddy.** One or more of the resource group members may also serve as process buddies for the session. The process buddy assists and supports the group through attention to logistics (supplies, materials, clean flip chart paper ready, monitoring the group process, and so on). The process buddy is, in many ways, an "assistant facilitator" during the session.

Supplementary Pages

In addition to the Messy Situation pages, the following three pages can be used to help remind students of the general stages in the CPS process and to help group members apply any of the stages during a working session. They are not intended as workbook pages in which the students work individually to write down "correct" answers for each section. Instead, use them as process guides or prompts to help a working session move along smoothly for any of the CPS stages or components you are applying. These supplementary pages can be duplicated for use with any of the 50 Messy Situations in Section III. A number of other extensions of or variations on these three basic pages can also be found in *The Creative Problem Solver's Guidebook* (3rd ed.; Treffinger, 2000a).

Data

For a Messy Situation, you can gather data to help you with problem solving.

Know	Need or Want to Know

Problem

Use the Data you've uncovered to make several possible problem statements.

In What Ways Might ... or How Might ...

Figure 2: Data & Problem

Choose a problem statement that you can use to generate many, interesting, and unusual ideas. **In what ways might** _____

_____

Idea

For your problem statement, generate as many ideas as you can.

Solution

Think of a number of criteria to use to help you compare, improve, or evaluate your ideas. Write your criteria here:

Choose the most important criteria, then use them to analyze your ideas. What ideas (or combinations of ideas) are most promising?

Figure 3: Idea & Solution

Acceptance

Use the questions "Who? What? When? Where? Why? and How?" to help you turn your most promising ideas into useful ones.

Assisters	Resisters

Plan of Action

Now, write out your Plan. Be as specific and detailed as possible.

1. (24-hour step)

2.

3.

4.

5.

6.

Figure 4: Acceptance & Plan of Action

Some Specific "Tips"

When you do use the CPS practice problems, several additional "tips" will help your teaching or training efforts to be effective. These include:

1. Use large newsprint or flipchart paper to write down the group's ideas. While each group member may have a practice problem booklet consisting of the Messy Situation and the additional three process pages, you will certainly find the group's thinking will be aided by sharing ideas with each other and by seeing all the ideas as they work together on the task. Also, if you are working with one CPS component or stage, but intend to work with one or more of the other components at a later time, the sheets will be helpful to save. When you continue your work later, put the sheets back up. Large sheets can be viewed easily, and they help members of the group "refresh their minds" about the previous work that was done with the problem.

2. When you are working on the problem, write down every idea and do not be concerned with detailed editing. A CPS session is not a grammar lesson. Don't make it into one.

3. Refrain from putting in your own ideas during a session. This often suggests to students that you are giving them "the right answer" or the ideas they are supposed to choose. Let the students do the thinking.

4. Feel free to use active learning methods, such as role-playing, socio-drama, or creative dramatics, and to add tools such as imagery, SCAMPER, or analogies when the group works on a practice problem. There is no one best way to deal with any of the problems.

5. After you have finished working with a group on any of the practice problems, take some time to talk together about the process methods and tools that you used. Discuss the students' feelings and reactions to the content of the problem and the solution(s) they developed. Since the goal is primarily to build their competence and confidence in using the CPS process, be certain to focus on what happened during the session. First, discuss what went well or what was best about the session. Second, answer any process questions they may have (why a certain tool was used, or what stages were confusing). Third, ask what the limitations or weaknesses of the session were, and try to think of some ways of overcoming each one in the future. Time for reflection and discussion of the process builds metacognitive skills and helps set the stage for effective transfer and application of CPS.

After Practicing CPS: What Comes Next?

As students or trainees become skillful, confident creative problem solvers, they will quickly become eager to work on some real life opportunities and challenges—situations that truly matter to them, have direct consequences for them, and for which they will really carry out their Action Plans. (See Figure 1, in Section I.)

Look for opportunities to help the students get started on real challenges. For students, these might include such immediate concerns as individual projects, group or classroom projects, school or community problems to be solved, or opportunities to apply CPS in such challenges as inventing new products. For adult trainees, real problems are the personal or professional challenges that are most important to them—the challenges or concerns about which the participants really seek new ideas or effective solutions.

Thus, the CPS practice problems in this book are intermediate resources in helping people become proficient in applying CPS. They are more complex and challenging than basic exercises for "creative" or "divergent" thinking, and they will prepare the group to move into complex real life challenges with confidence and skill.

We also invite you (and your students) to create some new Messy Situations for us to consider including in future collections and to send us information about real problems you have solved using CPS.

Section III:
The CPS Practice Problems

The CPS practice problems included in this book are:

- Always Starting
- Baby-Sitting Brats
- Bored
- Bowling
- Broken Eggs
- Bus Ride
- Business Sense
- But I Didn't
- Chew Stop
- Chores
- Food, Food, Food
- Fort
- Gone Fishing
- Gourmet
- Hockey Sticks
- Homesick
- Homework Helper
- Jars
- Keep It Cool
- Leaves
- Messy Lockers
- A MONOPOLY®
- More $$$
- New Bike
- New Club

- New Games
- New Holidays
- Nursery Rhymes
- Old Toys
- Paint
- Paper
- Party!
- Pet Exerciser
- Playground
- The Popular Vote
- Privacy!
- Responsible
- Sitcom
- Sleepy
- Smoke Out
- Snow
- Something Special
- Super Popular Toy
- Time Conflict
- TV Executive
- Twins
- Uniquely You
- We're Musical!
- Will It Fly?
- The Winner

ALWAYS STARTING

Messy Situation

Many people, young and old, have sometimes had a problem finishing a project they have started. Some people have more trouble finishing things than others. It is common for these people to begin many projects, but to finish none or only a few of them. Do you know anyone like this?

Your challenge is to plan a rehabilitation course (a helpful plan or program) that will turn these "starters" into "finishers."

What kinds of incentives or rewards would help them finish projects?

What type of organization or structure would help them finish?

Can you create any practice exercises or activities that would help them become better finishers?

Find out all you can about "starters" and plan a program that will turn a "starter" into a "finisher." A person would be considered a "starter" if he or she finishes less than half of the projects started. People would be considered "finishers" if at least 75% of their projects are finished within a reasonable time.

(Don't forget to consider how you will determine whether or not your program or plan is successful.)

BABY-SITTING BRATS

Messy Situation

You have just started baby-sitting this month. It seemed like a good idea because you need more spending money of your own, and you live in a neighborhood where there are lots of children, so there are plenty of baby-sitting opportunities.

The place where you are supposed to work tonight is a five-minute walk from your home. The parents of the children go out quite often, so you know they could really become good customers for you. There are three children in the family: a girl 7 years old and twin boys who are 4 years old. You know the children are supposed to be in bed by 8 p.m., and the parents said they will give you the phone number and address where they can be reached in case of an emergency. However, you've already heard from several of your friends that these children are very difficult to handle. Throughout the neighborhood, they have the reputation of being real brats.

One of your friends told you about some really terrible experiences with these children: They kicked, yelled, screamed, and refused to go to bed when they were supposed to. They held on to chairs and other pieces of furniture when your friend tried to carry them and really made a mess of the house. The boys ran around the house, screaming and knocking into furniture, and their sister told her parents, untruthfully, that your friend hit the boys and caused the bruises that they got by running into things.

You want to take the job because you really need the money. Since these people go out often, they pay top rates. But, you're certainly worried and nervous about the terrible time these children might give you. You want to do a good job so you will make a good impression and have them call you again.

What might you do about this Mess?

BORED

Messy Situation

Each year you look forward to your summer vacation. You plan good times with your friends, with lots of time for sports and hobbies, time to swim and lie on the beach, and just have a great time without thinking about schoolwork at all for the whole summer.

The trouble is: it's now just two weeks since summer vacation started, and you have already seen all your friends, played all those great summer sports, swam, and basked in the sun on the beach, and run out of ideas for new hobbies.

As happens each year at this time, you are already totally bored with summer fun. You have done all the things that you planned to do, and it wasn't nearly as wonderful as you imagined. You've completely run out of ideas for things to do.

You don't know why this happens every year, but it does, regardless of your plans and enthusiasm before vacation begins. Once you have been to the beach, or played softball or volleyball a few dozen times, they just don't seem to be much fun anymore. What might be done about this Mess? There are eight more weeks of vacation left, and you don't want to spend them being bored.

Develop a plan to deal with summer boredom. You might consider ways to prevent this problem from happening, or new and interesting ways to deal with it when it does happen.

BOWLING

Messy Situation

You enjoy going bowling on Saturdays with your friends. You belong to a team, and you're one of the better bowlers on it. It took a lot of practice for you to learn this sport, and you are proud of your bowling skill. Some of the other members on the team look up to you as a good bowler and an asset to the team.

One Saturday during the championship tournament, when your team particularly needs a strike or a spare, you are the one on whom they are depending. It is all up to you. You are very nervous because the whole team depends on you and they really need to win this game in the tournament. Your hands begin to sweat because of your nervousness. You wipe them again and again, but they keep getting sweaty. You do not get a good grip on the ball because of the sweat and, as you release it, the ball bounces on the alley and goes into the gutter.

You hear the astonished groans of your teammates as they realize you have thrown a gutterball. The noise of the bouncing ball attracts the attention of other bowlers, and everyone is staring at you. You are embarrassed, and that is making you even more nervous. You must do something before your next shot to prevent a repeat of the gutterball and save the game for your team. The harder you try to relax, the more nervous you become and the wetter your hands get. What might you be able to do to control your nerves in a tight spot like this? Develop a unique and detailed plan to handle this situation (or other similar situations).

BROKEN EGGS

Messy Situation

Have you ever gone shopping alone or with a member of your family? Have you ever included eggs in the things you are purchasing and bringing home? Have you ever checked the eggs in the store and found that some of them are cracked in the carton? Have you or has anyone you know ever dropped the egg carton on the way to the car or on the way into the house? What happens to the eggs? Do the egg cartons protect the eggs adequately, or are they damaged when they 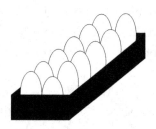 are dropped? Do you think it is important to protect the eggs from damage if the carton is dropped? Many people who have lost some or all of the eggs that they purchased think that the egg cartons should provide more protection for the eggs. Store owners have a high loss of eggs from dropping of the cartons in shipping or in stocking the shelves, and they would welcome a plan to reduce these losses. Can you help them by designing a better egg carton?

Your challenge is to design a new egg carton that will do a better job of protecting the eggs from damage if the carton is dropped. You cannot use a traditional egg carton. Usually, eggs are accidentally dropped from no more than waist height. Your carton should protect the eggs if dropped from that height. Design, construct, and test your "new and improved" egg carton. How will you decide if your solution really is better than the ordinary cartons?

BUS RIDE

Messy Situation

You are in charge of the activities for the bus ride to the class field trip. The length of the bus ride for this year's trip is two hours to the site and two hours to return. You must plan activities so that your classmates will not become bored and the bus driver will not be disturbed. Some of the trip will take the bus through high traffic areas where the driver needs relative quiet to concentrate on driving and following a complicated route.
Another part of the trip, however, will be over clear and open roads. During this part of the trip quiet is not as necessary and the driver would not be distracted by some "reasonable noise" from the students on the bus.

On previous occasions, there have been group games for everyone on the bus to play, and these usually worked pretty well. But, you don't want to do the same things, so try to find some new and different possibilities.

Your challenge is to plan some activities for the students that are fun, safe, and interesting. Some of the activities should provide entertainment in a quiet way, and some of the activities can be noisier. (Suggestion for a possible "test" of your solution: When you have completed your plan for the trip to the site and back, try out some of your solutions with a group of students from your school who will be taking a field trip. Interview the students, teachers or chaperones, and the bus driver to determine the success of your plan.)

BUSINESS SENSE

Messy Situation

Many people have started new businesses and been successful. Part of the traditional "American Dream" has been to start a business through which one can become very successful (and perhaps even wealthy).

Have you ever thought about starting a business of your own? Would it be something you would do on your own, or would a group of people join you? What would be the nature of the business? Would it provide goods or services? What type of people would use your business? How could you plan for a business venture, alone or with a group, that would quickly become very successful?

Your challenge is to think of a unique and interesting new business venture (alone or with a group). You will need to do plenty of "Exploring Data" to get started, not only to decide what kind of business venture to begin, but also to be sure you have a good plan, in which you've considered many important decisions that must be made in beginning a business. You will discover that there are many books and pamphlets on this subject, and there will certainly also be many organizations and individuals in your area from whom you should get information before you proceed.

Your only limitations are the laws of your area. Your business idea must be legal. It should also become profitable in a short period of time for you, your group, or your school.

Perhaps you will even decide to follow through on your plan and start the business in your area.

BUT I DIDN'T

Messy Situation

How many times can you remember being scolded and blamed for something you didn't do? Was it a brother, sister, friend, or other student who was involved?

Sometimes, you really know who the guilty party is, and sometimes you don't. Either way, you often find yourself in a no-win situation. If you know who is really guilty, you may not be able to prove it. You may not want to reveal the identity of the guilty party, or you may not know who really did it. In any case, you often find yourself saying, "But I didn't ..." even though the person in charge, (your mother or father, or a teacher, for example) does not believe you.

What should you do in this case? Plan a number of tactics to follow in the event that you are not believed. The tactics might be different for different circumstances (i.e., what to do when you don't want to reveal the guilty person, what to do when you don't know who the guilty person is, and so on). Make up a "survival guide" for young people who are not believed when they should be.

CHEW STOP

Messy Situation

Your family has a pet dog that you like very much. There is only one problem with your pet: He is a 5-year-old beagle who has never outgrown the chewing stage. When he was a puppy, he chewed up shoes, socks, and hats belonging to the whole family. He seems to have outgrown his liking for shoes and socks, but not for hats. Since you spend a lot of time with him, he seems to be particularly attracted to your hats.

You like hats and have a lot of them. You collect them from different places. Many of them go with particular outfits or are just "special" to you for one reason or another. Your dog also likes hats, but he prefers chewing them to wearing or collecting them!

Each time you leave your door open, another one of your hats will be damaged by your pet. Locking the door deters him, but it is a nuisance to lock the door each time you go in or out. If you leave the door open, even for only a few minutes, you can be assured that your pet will get into the room and start chewing on a hat.

What can you do about this Mess?

CHORES

Messy Situation

Making your bed each day is a chore that many people would like to avoid. It is time consuming and boring. It takes time that you could be using to do something more interesting. The bed just gets messed up again each night anyway! It is one of those dull, routine chores that we must do each day, over and over again.

Washing the dishes is another, similar time-consuming chore that we must do each day, and often more than once a day. The dishes never stay clean. As soon as we have them all done, someone in the family will want a drink or a snack and get them dirty again. We just never seem to get finished with it. It just wastes our precious time.

Think of all the things you could do with the time spent on these chores *if* you could find a special way to do them more easily, more quickly, and more efficiently—or maybe even eliminate them so they would never have to be done again. Think of how nice it would be to have all the dishes clean and the beds made without your having to spend all those hours of time and effort!

Your challenge is to devise a way of accomplishing your chores and also having time for yourself. Choose any daily boring chore you want and find a way to control it successfully (or maybe even eliminate it). Make a unique presentation that will convince others of the practicality and benefits of your plan.

FOOD, FOOD, FOOD

Messy Situation

Every day, throughout the world, restaurants throw away a great amount of uneaten food. Public health laws prevent them from reserving or reusing this food, and, for similar reasons, they cannot simply give it away to hungry people.

Even if it can't be served and eaten, there might be a number of other creative ways to use this discarded food.

Your challenge in this problem is to consider new and unusual uses for discarded, uneaten food and to develop a promising solution for this problem.

FORT

Messy Situation

Many restaurants, movie theaters, stores, and other commercial buildings are designed and decorated with a theme in mind. For example, stores that sell fresh seafood are very often decorated with a nautical theme. Many steak houses are built and decorated with a Western theme to suggest cattle ranches and cowboys. The shape, color, furnishings, and wall decorations all contribute to creating the desired image, mood, or theme for the building.

Suppose you were planning a clubhouse or fort for a new club. Plan how you would build and decorate the fort to create a theme that best represents the nature and goals of your club.

Your problem-solving challenge is to think about how you can best make the design of your fort show clearly what your club is about.

When you have decided on your solution, you can make a detailed drawing or construct a model, or perhaps actually construct the fort. Use only materials you can find readily at home or school. Your product should demonstrate what makes your solution unusual, interesting, and especially appropriate for your club. Remember, the fort or clubhouse should show the theme or mood that you have chosen to create for your club.

GONE FISHING

Messy Situation

For several days, as usual, your father has been talking about wanting you to go fishing with him this weekend. He says the fish will be biting and just waiting for you both to catch them. You and your dad don't get to spend too much time together, and you really appreciate his thought, but ... your dad is a great fisherman. He is always able to catch the most and biggest fish on any fishing trip with you or with his friends. You know that he has asked you because he loves to fish and because he wants to spend time with you. He is busy most of the week with his job, so you don't get to see a lot of each other.

He started taking you along on his weekend fishing trips a few years ago and has invested quite a bit of money into equipment for the two of you. You have all the best in tackle and equipment, but you are not good at fishing. Your dad's skill and interest in the sport has increased. Your skill has remained at the beginner stage, and your interest has been reduced to absolute boredom. Each time you go fishing, you never catch any fish and you are totally bored. The time and opportunity to be with your dad and talk together is important to you, but you wish there were another way.

Lately, you have become so bored on these fishing excursions that you haven't even been able to enjoy the time. Your dad is always landing the big ones while you just sit there. You might enjoy the trips if you caught fish, but you don't know for sure because you never catch any. This weekend, there is an activity at your school that you could use for an excuse. It is not something that you really care a lot about, but it wouldn't be as boring as fishing. The last three times your dad has asked you about fishing, however, you have made up an excuse. You fear that he may be suspicious, and you don't want to hurt his feelings. But, you don't think you can stand another whole weekend of boredom.

The weatherman just predicted a beautiful weekend ahead, and your dad is making preparations for the trip. What are you going to do about this Mess?

GOURMET

Messy Situation

Have you ever had a gourmet meal? Did you enjoy it? What do we mean by a gourmet meal? Have you noticed that, in different restaurants, each chef has a favorite dish or specialty that he or she prepares? This special meal or dish is unique in that it is the chef's personal recipe or design for combining food to make a special meal.

Suppose you were a famous gourmet chef whose specialty is something that many people (and especially young people) don't like. Design a chef's specialty that reflects your unique specialty and your unique ideas for convincing people to try it and enjoy it.

Plan how you would prepare the food, how the food would be arranged or presented on the plate, and how you might convince people that it's really a great thing to eat!

When your plan is complete, you might even carry it out and serve your special meal to someone. You will know that you have been successful when the people who eat your special meal enjoy it. (Are there some other criteria you might also use to help you determine how successful you were?)

HOCKEY STICKS

Messy Situation

Broken hockey sticks are an abundant resource. The game of hockey is an action-packed, contact sport, and, in the normal course of a game, many sticks are broken. Each year, thousands of hockey sticks are purchased, broken, and discarded. This is a tremendous waste of material. Do you have any broken hockey sticks at home? Collect some sticks from home or from friends who are avid hockey players. What other uses might you find for these broken sticks?

Your challenge is to devise a useful purpose for broken hockey sticks.

If your new purpose or use will become part or all of a completely new object, you must make a model or prototype of the object to illustrate the new use.

If you reuse the broken sticks as they are, then you must demonstrate this use.

Make sure that you consider a specific consumer group or audience (children, senior citizens, and so forth) who will find your product especially interesting and useful, either now or in the future.

Try to think up a really exciting, interesting, and innovative use!

HOMESICK

Messy Situation

You are at summer camp for the first time. You have never been to this camp before, but it was your idea to come. For months, you have looked forward to your two weeks at camp. The camp is everything it was advertised to be. It's large, very beautiful, and has every sport and recreation facility you could ask for. You're all set for two fun-filled weeks, but …

The trouble starts after the third day. You have made several new friends, but you are starting to miss your best friends from home. You like the other people assigned to your cabin, but the bunk bed just isn't like your bed at home. You miss your parents and even your bratty little brother or sister. Since you had never been away from home for any long period of time before, you never considered the possibility that you might become homesick. You have spent a lot of time at home proving to everyone how grown up you are, and now this happens. It might ruin everything!

What will you do? You still have a week and a half at camp, and you are already so homesick you want to leave. But, you can't admit it to your family. What is your plan for the rest of the camp session?

HOMEWORK HELPER

Messy Situation

Invent a new system, a plan, or a machine, tool, or device that will help you with getting your homework done promptly, accurately, and efficiently. Your invention might help you with any aspect of the important (but not always pleasant) business of doing homework.

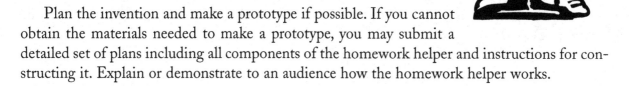

The invention must be new. It cannot be a product that is already on the market, and you must use reasonable care to determine that you are not using the idea of another inventor. However, the invention may be a combination of parts of other inventions or products. The invention should be useful in doing homework. You may choose a certain subject area for which it will be particularly useful, a grade level of students for whom it might be especially valuable, or you may do it as a general or "all-purpose" homework helper.

Plan the invention and make a prototype if possible. If you cannot obtain the materials needed to make a prototype, you may submit a detailed set of plans including all components of the homework helper and instructions for constructing it. Explain or demonstrate to an audience how the homework helper works.

Remember to consider ways to determine your success in solving the problem.

JARS

Messy Situation

Do you know what "canning" food means? Many of your grandparents, and perhaps your parents, as well, used to prepare canned fruits and vegetables so they could be available throughout the year, not just when they were in season and readily available at the store. Modern transportation and refrigeration has made it possible today for us to obtain a wide selection of fresh fruits and vegetables throughout the year, of course. But, some people have continued to "can" foods anyway because they enjoy preparing things themselves. Canning food can be hard work, and it requires plenty of time, too.

Your mother has decided to give up canning. She's too busy, canning takes too much of her time, and everything she used to can is just as easy to get at the store anyway. Through the years, however, she has invested a large amount of money in the jars and other things needed for canning. Now, she has absolutely no use for them. She will give you all the jars and supplies if you can think of a good use for them. You have four cases of jars (with 24 jars in each case). There are two sizes (a quart and a pint, because these jars were made before the use of Metric measures became popular). There are metal rings and tops for all the jars. Find alternate uses for them.

You may modify the jars in any way possible for you, but you must do all the work. Your teacher or parent may show you how to do something, but they may not do it for you. You may use all four cases of jars, or just as many as you need. You must produce a new product that is marketable. (It must be something that someone would want to buy.) You may add other materials to the jars or use other materials in making your final product. The value of the additional materials you use may not be more than $5. You may use materials you already have or purchase them, but the total value may not exceed $5. Plan the product or other use of the jars, and make one sample item to illustrate your plan.

KEEP IT COOL

Messy Situation

Are you an ice cream lover? Do you have an ice cream lover in your family or do you know one? True ice cream lovers are seldom without a source of their favorite cold treat. They can buy it at the supermarket or at specialty stores that offer dozens of different flavors. Many stores offer you the choice of eating it right there, on the spot, or taking a package home to eat later. Ice cream lovers seldom have a problem finding a place to purchase their favorite dessert—but when the weather is very warm, they do sometimes have trouble getting it home safely. Have you ever returned home from the store with a package of ice cream on a hot summer day and found the package already starting to melt and drip before you could get it to the freezer?

Ice cream is usually packaged in cardboard containers that are very attractive and do an excellent job of showing you what flavor is hidden inside. The containers do not always do such a good job, however, of keeping the ice cream cold and solid for the trip from the store to your house.

What might you be able to do about this?

Design a packaging system for ice cream that will prevent it from getting soft or melting and dripping all over you for at least a 30-minute trip from the store to your home in typical hot summer conditions (approximately 75° Fahrenheit). Make a "prototype" of your solution and test it in a 75° F room.

(This problem may well require some background research!)

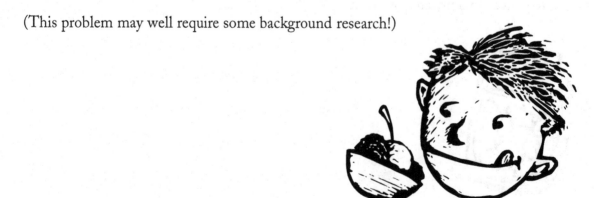

LEAVES

Messy Situation

You have just spent three hours raking the leaves from your neighbor's large yard. You have raked them all into three large piles near the road for the garbage collectors to pick up. When you go to the house to be paid for your work, the owner tells you that there's just been a news bulletin on TV: The garbage collectors have gone on strike and will not collect the leaves. The neighbor reminds you that you were hired to remove the leaves, so the job is not really finished until the leaves are gone. Since the garbage collectors will not pick up the leaves, you are responsible for them. Your neighbor will not pay you until you have finished the whole job, which includes removing the leaves. You will not get paid for all your work until you think of something to do with three very large piles of leaves.

There is a law in your town that forbids the burning of leaves in an open fire. Your parents certainly won't let you bring the leaves to your yard. How might you get rid of or use in some new and unusual ways those three big piles of leaves?

MESSY LOCKERS

Messy Situation

Do you have a locker or a desk at school in which you store your books and some personal belongings? How neat is your locker or desk? Is it ever messy and hard to arrange or find things? If your locker or desk is always neat, do you have a friend who has a messy locker or desk? Have you ever seen a locker or desk that is so messy or disorganized that it would take a year to find anything in it? Have you ever needed something in a hurry and not been able to find it in your locker or a friend's messy locker? What plan or organizational design could help in this situation?

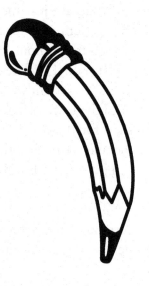

Your challenge is to create a design, plan, method, system, or object that will help you find things in a messy locker. Your solution might be a "permanent" solution (which could be used all the time), or an "emergency" strategy or device (for special situations when you need to find something in a hurry). It must be easy and efficient.

When your plan is complete, try it on the messiest locker that you know of and see if you are successful.

A MONOPOLY®

(close to home!)

Messy Situation

MONOPOLY has been a tremendously successful game. Generations of people have played and enjoyed the game, passed "Go," and collected $200. The MONOPOLY game could be improved, brought up to date, and made more relevant for your own area. Think of many ways that would make it more modern and exciting.

Your challenge in this problem is to redo the game of MONOPOLY. Make a working model of your new version, using pieces from the old game and parts that you make. Get reactions from several people who volunteer to try out the new game. Good luck!

Some suggestions for Exploring Data:

What are the major parts of the game? What might need to be changed, made more modern, or brought closer to home for each part? (New utilities? Modern transportation? New kinds of places to live? New cards? New street names or places? Modern prices? New entertainment?)

What new situations, rules, or strategies would also add an up-to-date element to the game?

 # MORE $$$

Messy Situation

Everything seems to cost more these days! You have decided that you need more money, and a substantial increase in your weekly allowance would be just great. Last week, you put in a request to your parents for the additional money, but they refused. Since they believe an increase is not necessary, they politely refused your polite request for the money. They may be right, but you've decided that, if you had a better plan, you might have a greater chance of success in getting the raise.

Your challenge, then, is to find a really new and effective way to increase your weekly income by the amount that you requested for the increase in your allowance. This doesn't have to be a plan for getting a raise in your allowance, of course. That's only one way to look at the situation. Your goal in this challenge is simply a greater weekly income.

To deal with this Mess, you may have to look at some things in new and different ways, not just asking your parents for more money. You should consider your goals, needs, and many ways to increase your income. Your Plan of Action should be very specific (not just, "I'll get a job after school").

You're trying to develop a plan for increasing your weekly income by a certain amount you've set as your goal (or maybe by even more than your minimum goal). Good thinking! (If you're a huge success with your plan, will we all get a commission?)

NEW BIKE

Messy Situation

You really want a new 10-speed bike this year. You already have a bike, but it is an old three-speed, and you want a better one. When you approached your parents with the suggestion that they get you a 10-speed bike, they didn't understand. They said that the bike you already have is fine for transportation, and the new one you want is just too expensive for them to afford at this time.

You have already picked out the bike that you want. The color is just perfect—and you have always wanted a 10-speed. You can just imagine yourself speeding along on the sleek new bike. You stop at the bike shop often to look at it. You love bicycle riding, and you would like one day to compete in a real bike race.

You have a few dollars saved from doing odd jobs, but your allowance seems to be gone the minute you get it. At the rate you can save your money, you'd be old and ready to retire before you could buy the bike. There aren't too many jobs available, and you can't get a regular-paying job after school. You don't have even half the price of the new bike. You're going to need all your Creative Problem Solving skills to come up with some really new ways of getting that bike.

Good luck with your creative thinking!

NEW CLUB

Messy Situation

Young people in many countries throughout the world belong to clubs. They are drawn together because of common interests, abilities, or other factors. What are some of the common interests that you share with some friends that might cause you to want to get together with others to form a club?

Plan a club that is based on a particular theme or interest area.

Your final product for solving this problem should be a detailed plan for a new club. Remember, many details will have to be considered when you are "Exploring Data" (for example, such things as members, officers, meeting places, times, content and goals of the club, and so forth). Keep in mind the theme or interest area, too.

What kind of new club might produce the most interest and enthusiasm in your school? What can you do, and how will you know if you've succeeded?

# NEW GAMES

Messy Situation

Pat and Chris are 10 years old. They have kept many games and puzzles that they have received as gifts throughout their lives. One by one, each game becomes boring to them. As soon as they learn the rules and play each game a number of times, they become bored. They are looking for a solution for this. They have lots of time alone at home when their parents are busy or not available. They are bored with the usual television programs, so they're looking for an interesting and enjoyable way to spend their time.

They live in a small community, within walking distance of each other. They are free to occupy their time with the resources that they have, but it's difficult for them to get to sources of entertainment in town. Their parents will allow them to go to each other's houses to play, but will not drive them into the center of town to the movies or arcades. They have the following resources:

- many old games and toys;
- tape;
- paste;
- paints and paint supplies;
- scissors;
- paper, rubber bands, cloth, and other items found in the house; and
- time and good imaginations.

Your challenge is to design a game for Pat and Chris using the same resources that they have. (If an item is usually found around the house, you can use it.) Try to design a game that will not become boring for them as quickly as their other games.

NEW HOLIDAYS

Messy Situation

We all have traditional ways of celebrating our holidays, such as: Thanksgiving turkey, Halloween costumes, and fireworks on the Fourth of July (in the U.S.).

Choose any holiday that is (or should be) celebrated in the United States, Canada, or another country of your choice. The list below will get you started in thinking about some of these holidays. For this problem, you might use one of these holidays, or you might prefer to select a different one of your own.

- Groundhog Day
- Labor Day
- Confederation Day
- Memorial Day
- April Fool's Day

- St. Patrick's Day
- Valentine's Day
- Independence Day
- Columbus Day
- Dominion Day

Find as much information as you can about the holiday. How is it usually celebrated? Why do we celebrate it? Where (or how or why) did it originate? Is it celebrated in different ways in various places?

Then, design a new way to celebrate the holiday. Plan a fresh, creative new way to celebrate the holiday you have chosen. Try to make your plan for the celebration both meaningful and enjoyable so people will look forward to it.

Develop a way to test your plan.

NURSERY RHYMES

Messy Situation

Many of you remember a number of the nursery rhymes you learned as a child. ("Hickory, dickory, dock, the mouse ran up the clock," and so forth.) Think of the many rhymes you learned and enjoyed. Your challenge is to make a modern day nursery rhyme. You may adapt an existing rhyme or make an entirely new one. The rhyme should be rhythmical and easy to learn. It should incorporate things that are common in our modern culture and that the children of today will recognize. It should be short and easy for young children to learn, and it also should be something that they will enjoy.

When you have developed your new rhyme, plan a way to present it to young children. You could include a skit, costumes, music, or other options in your presentation. Remember that your audience of young children must enjoy the rhyme and the presentation. You know that you have been successful if the listening audiences remembers the rhyme and can repeat at least a few lines of your rhyme on their own.

OLD TOYS

Messy Situation

What do you do with the toys that you have outgrown or that have been broken? Do you still have any around your house that you or your brothers or sisters have broken or outgrown? Sometimes these old toys are kept around at home for sentimental reasons or because we think that, sometime in the future, we will fix them, reuse them, or give them to someone else. Sometimes, they just get pushed to the back of the closet and are forgotten.

Have the members of your class gather and bring in all the pieces and parts of old, broken toys that they can find. Then, using only these parts, imagine some new combinations and uses. How could you use these pieces and parts to put together a new toy for someone your age or other young people?

Your challenge is to make, from the materials in your class collection, a new and unique toy, one that young people your age (or younger) would use and enjoy. The new toy must be made primarily of the pieces and parts of old, outgrown, or broken toys. You may use tape, glue, screws, wire, and so on to assemble your toy, but its main components must be pieces from the old, broken, or outgrown toys that have been collected. Try to make your toy new or different—unlike other toys you have seen.

When you have constructed your new toy, plan to present it to a group of young people who might use and enjoy it. Demonstrate the new toy to your target audience and get their reactions.

PAINT

Messy Situation

You hate the color of your room. You have hated it for some time now, but your parents are unwilling to repaint it now simply because you cannot stand the color. It will be repainted with the whole house in two or three years, they say.

One weekend, while your parents are away, you are looking through some junk in the basement when you come upon some old cans of paint. They are just the perfect color that you'd love to use for your room. There seems to be plenty of paint to cover your room. You decide to paint the room and surprise your parents upon their return.

You cover all the furniture very carefully and begin the job. When you have two and one-half walls painted, you open the last can and find that it has only a tiny bit of paint in it. You will run out of paint before you can finish the third wall—and there's another whole wall to do after that! You return to the basement, but there is no more paint of that color. In fact, there's not enough paint of any color in the basement to cover your whole room. The remaining cans are all small quantities of several colors.

Next, you call the paint store and learn that the paint you used was a special mixture that cannot be matched any longer. You would have had enough money to buy paint to finish the remaining walls of the room if it could have been matched, but not to buy enough paint to repaint the whole room. It is Saturday afternoon and your parents will return late Sunday night. What will you do?

PAPER

Messy Situation

How many sheets of paper did you use in school today? Don't forget the paper on which you took notes, scratch paper, test paper, copy paper, art paper, and probably several other kinds, as well. What happened to the paper after you were finished with it? How full is your classroom waste basket after a normal day? What happens to all that paper? Are there any other options for that paper other than throwing it all away?

Some schools have turned used paper into money with paper drives. But, they can usually only do that a few times each year in most places. How about the wasted paper during the rest of the year? Having a paper drive is only one of the many possible uses of scrap paper. Think of all the types of scrap paper you normally have in your classroom or school and try to find some alternative uses for this paper.

Your challenge is to devise a new and unusual use for normal school scrap paper. Your solution should be designed for the types of scrap paper that you normally have in your school.

When you have decided on your new use for your school's waste paper, prepare a presentation for your teacher, class, or principal to convince them of the value of the new use and also to persuade them to use the paper in this new way.

PARTY!

Messy Situation

Next week is your best friend's birthday. You want to have the best birthday party ever, one that your friend will never forget. You want this party to be unlike any other party that has ever been held because your friend is better than any other friend. Your friend will be 15 in two weeks. What will the party be like?

As you plan your friend's birthday celebration, you have a few limitations that you must consider. You have only $5 to spend, and the birthday is two weeks away. You may, of course, use anything that you can obtain for free or that you can get people to donate for the celebration. You may use any services, materials, and so forth that you can obtain for $5 or less in order to put together the greatest birthday celebration that there ever was. Don't forget that everything—whatever is part of your solution for the party—must fit within these limits.

(When you have your plan completed, perhaps you could actually hold a real celebration for someone to test the plan.)

PET EXERCISER

Messy Situation

Many people today live in apartments, town houses, and other dwellings that have either no yards or very small yards. Many of these people have pets, and exercising them has become a modern day problem.

People today live very busy lives and have less time to walk their pets. Letting pets run loose is impractical, dangerous, and even illegal in some places. Many families do not live where there are fenced yards. Everyone's at work or school all day. As a result, many pets just sit around the house all day getting little or no exercise.

Design a new way to exercise your pet. You may choose any pet you wish to exercise. Demonstrate your plan, method, or product.

PLAYGROUND

Messy Situation

Children need room to play and safe, enjoyable things to play with and on. For this reason, playgrounds have been built in many places in most communities in schools, parks, and sometimes in other places, as well. One of the interesting things about playgrounds is that they are designed for children—but seldom by children. What are the things you like about the playgrounds available to you? Are there any changes you would make if you, instead of an adult, were designing a playground?

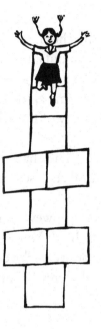

This is your chance! Design the perfect playground for children or young people. Plan what you want to have in the playground and where you might like to have it located. Plan where you might obtain the materials and things you want in the playground. In choosing a site, make sure that it is a place where young people would most benefit.

THE POPULAR VOTE

Messy Situation

Let's assume that you have never been the "most popular person" in school. You are not disliked by the other students, but with your own outside interests, you've never found the time to cultivate many close relationships with your schoolmates. You haven't tried to become an officer of any school clubs before, nor have you taken part in any of the school's most popular sports or extracurricular activities.

The chances are pretty good, then, that it wouldn't be easy for you to be elected to anything. In fact, it seems that the same few popular kids are always the ones getting elected.

However, in a club that you do belong to, there is a certain office that you would really love to hold. You would probably be the best qualified person for that job in the whole school, and you would love to do it, and you know you would do a great job. But, you're sure that someone who's really popular with everyone will come along and get it.

If you try to tell how well-qualified you are, other students might not be convinced, or they might just think you're bragging and vote for someone else.

Your challenge: Describe the club, the job, and come up with a really new and unusual plan for getting elected to that position.

PRIVACY!

Messy Situation

Have you ever been in a position where you felt that you had no privacy? Why did you feel that way? Was someone else always around when you wanted to do something that you thought should be private? Did it seem that you were never able to be by yourself, or to have things that you did not want to show to anyone?

This Messy Situation involves the issue of lack of privacy. Your family has just moved to another town, and your new home is smaller than the one you lived in before. You will now have to share a room with your nosy little brother or sister. There is not much chance that your family will be moving again soon or building any new additions onto the house, so your new room will probably have to do for a long time.

There are many private matters that you do not want to share with your sibling, but he or she has a habit of getting into your things when you are not around. In your old house, you could close the door to the room and ask him or her to stay out. This is no longer possible, of course. You also have times when you would like to have a friend over and talk in private. It seems that your brother/sister is always in or around your room every time. There are also times when you want quiet to study or think without anyone talking to you or asking you questions.

Devise a plan to ensure some privacy for yourself under these circumstances and a way that you could test whether the plan would work.

RESPONSIBLE

Messy Situation

Many young people would like to have more responsibility for planning their future (education, career, recreation, or other future choices or concerns). Students sometimes complain that adults (parents, teachers, or others) do not treat them as responsible, mature human beings, but rather as if they were babies.

On the other hand, parents and teachers often respond that the young people are not responsible and will harm themselves if they're allowed too much freedom in making choices in their lives. But, you must have some responsibility in order to demonstrate that you can handle it well!

Can you find a solution for this dilemma? Can students either become more responsible or demonstrate to adults that they are responsible? How might adults feel more secure about giving more responsibility to young people? How much responsibility should be given? How might some decisions be shared? How might adults be assured that the young people will not go "wild?"

Plan your solution for the part of this dilemma that you think is most challenging and devise a unique way to communicate your plan so that it will get the attention and support of adults.

Sitcom

Messy Situation

What are your favorite television shows? Are any of them situation comedies ("sitcoms")? Good television programming choices for young people today are pretty rare. See if you can do a better job of writing for television than the adults are doing.

Develop a plan for a totally new situation for a television comedy that you think will appeal to most everyone your age. Remember that your situation comedy must be really funny—so appealing to young people that they would tune in to watch it each week.

Plan your situation and develop a "pilot" program to test other students' reactions to your program. Present the pilot to a test audience of people of your age. The pilot program must introduce your regular characters and set the mood for future episodes.

Some Data to Consider:

Who are the characters? Who will be the "regulars"? What will be the situation that will bring these characters together? What are some new and unusual things that might happen to the characters? How will you be certain that the show will be funny?

Good thinking and lots of laughs!

SLEEPY

Messy Situation

Have you ever had to go to bed when you weren't sleepy? Was it because you had to get up especially early the next day? Or do your parents believe you should go to bed at a certain time regardless of whether or not you think you're sleepy?

Being in bed and not feeling sleepy can be frustrating to anyone, young or old. If you have been in bed for about 20 minutes or so, and you're still not sleepy, you usually start to feel frustrated, bored, and upset. What might you do about this?

Consider this situation: You are in bed. It is your usual bedtime, but you have been in bed for 30 minutes without falling asleep.

Tomorrow, your whole family is leaving on a trip about which you are very excited. You have been looking forward to the trip for months, and now the time is almost here. Your parents want to be ready to leave very early in the morning, so you must be up by 4:30 a.m. to help with the last-minute preparations. You want to be well-rested tomorrow so you won't miss any of the exciting events.

But, the harder you try to get to sleep, the more nervous and wide awake you feel. Your brother (or sister) who shares a room with you is asleep, and you are afraid that you will wake him or her if you keep tossing and turning. Even worse, you might wake your parents and make them angry. You've tried counting sheep, but it just doesn't seem to help.

What's the real problem in this situation? How would you deal with it?

SMOKE OUT

Messy Situation

What if the sale of cigarettes, cigars, and pipe tobacco were banned throughout the world? Huge tobacco companies have invested millions of dollars in the factories that produce cigarettes and cigars. These factories hire many people who would then be out of work. The machines that roll the tobacco and wrap paper around it to make cigarettes or cigars would become obsolete and perhaps might seem useless.

This would create tremendous problems: waste of the factories, machines, materials, and so on. We must also be concerned about jobs for all the people who worked in those plants. Our worldwide economy would certainly be hurt if this happened.

However, suppose that a unique new use could be found for the machines and factories. It would help reduce the waste of factories and equipment and could offer new employment for many of the people.

Don't be concerned about the technical details of how all this machinery really works. Think generally about the kinds of products and materials they involve: size, shape, materials, and so on.

Try to find one or more new and unusual product(s) that might be developed for the tobacco factories to manufacture. The use you select should produce a marketable product. Don't forget to consider how your new product might be promoted or "marketed" to the public.

SNOW

Messy Situation

Each winter, people throughout a large part of the world have a large supply of a certain raw material; snow. We shovel it out of our streets, driveways, and sidewalks and leave it in piles to melt away. Children have found some uses for this very abundant winter resource. They make snowmen, or have snowball fights, or build forts from snow. Some people make quite a profit by removing it for other people with plows, snow blowers, or shovels. There must be other ways we can use and profit from this unique resource.

Think of other uses for snow. You may add things to the snow to make objects, tools, displays, and so on, but the major part of your product must be snow. You can change the shape, form, and so forth, as long as your end product is made of snow in one form or another. Try to make a product that is useful and/or desirable to someone. Make something you could sell if it were properly advertised. Design the product, make it, and then outline the plan you would use to market it.

SOMETHING SPECIAL

Messy Situation

Mother's Day and Father's Day are usually celebrated by giving your mother or father a present or by doing something special on that day to show your appreciation and love for them.

It is one month from Mother's Day or Father's Day (choose the one you want to work with). You have a very limited budget, but you want to give your mother or father the best present ever. You have no other sources of money except the $2 you have saved.

Plan an ideal present for either Mother's Day or Father's Day. Whatever you plan must have a total cost of no more that $2, including all ingredients and parts that you must purchase. You may, however, use anything that you can salvage from scrap or find around the house.

Plan, construct, and wrap the "prefect present." Your limitations are the normal interests and tastes of your parent. The gift must be something that a parent would like to receive.

How might you ensure the success of your solution? How will you know how successful you've been in solving the problem?

SUPER POPULAR TOY

Messy Situation

The Hula Hoop® was a remarkable invention. Millions of people purchased and used the Hula Hoop® in the 1960s. It was simple to make and use, and it didn't require complex technology—or even batteries! Many people throughout the world derived enjoyment from their Hula Hoops®. The toy was used by children of all ages and even by adults. It was inexpensive to manufacture, and its appeal came from the fun that the people had with it. It did not require a large and expensive advertising campaign to sell the Hula Hoops®. Soon after their introduction to the public, many families had one—and some had two or three.

In the last few years, there have been many popular new toys each year. But, few have been as successful as the simple Hula Hoop®. Can you think of what would be the perfect new (but simple) "Super Popular Toy" for today? What might entertain both children and adults, and capture the toy market?

Design the super toy of the decade. Try to produce a prototype of your super toy. To make the prototype, you may use any materials that you can find around the house or school or any materials that you can obtain for free.

When you have produced the new toy, devise a clever plan to introduce it to the public and build its popularity.

TIME CONFLICT

Messy Situation

Let's assume that your family has one television set, but there are four people (you, your mother, your father, and one brother or sister). Everyone's always arguing and quarreling about who's going to be able to watch the TV and which program to watch. It seems that all four of you most often want to watch something different. Not even an expensive VCR can record four different programs at the very same time. It would be too expensive (and not very likely, anyway) for every member of the family to have his or her own TV set. But, you are really tired of missing some of the programs that you like the most because other family members want to watch other things at the same time that your program is on. You've tried sharing times by making a schedule for everyone, but that never seems to work very well.

So, your challenge is to devise a really creative new plan that will enable you and your family members to enjoy watching TV without so much conflict about whose time or turn it is.

TV Executive

Messy Situation

Your company has just negotiated a successful takeover of one of the major television networks, ABC, NBC, CBS, or Fox. You are the one who will design the new fall line-up of programs for this year. Your challenge is to design a fall schedule that will draw the most viewers and provide quality programming.

Choose a network, (ABC, NBC, CBS, or Fox) and look at the existing programs for "prime time" (8 p.m. to 11 p.m. Sunday through Saturday). You may use any of the existing shows that your network already has on its schedule and/or add any new shows that you want. You may also alter the format, stars, times, or length of any of the programs.

Ratings are determined by the size of the audience you are able to attract; advertisers want to do business with a network that has the highest ratings. So, you are going to have to devise a schedule that will draw the largest number of viewers. You can also include in your schedule specials and other events.

How will you determine what different people want to watch and arrange your schedule to please them? When your schedule is finished, choose a group of people and ask them to help test your ideas. They might check those shows they would watch or indicate to you in some other ways if they like your schedule.

TWINS

Messy Situation

You have new baby twin brothers. They are as cute as can be, and everyone loves them. You think they are cute, too (as cute as babies can be), and you like them enough since they are your brothers. The only problem is that, since they arrived, they have been getting all the attention from everyone who used to give you a lot of attention.

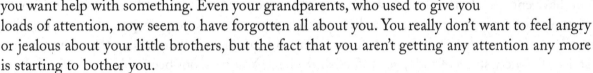

The twins are all the family talks about when they get together. Your parents seem to spend all their free time with the twins, when before there was time for them to spend with you. It seems as if your dad doesn't have any time to talk to you anymore, and your mom is constantly busy with the twins when you want help with something. Even your grandparents, who used to give you loads of attention, now seem to have forgotten all about you. You really don't want to feel angry or jealous about your little brothers, but the fact that you aren't getting any attention any more is starting to bother you.

What might be some constructive things you can do about this situation?

UNIQUELY YOU!

Messy Situation

You've decided that you really want a new, more stylish look or appearance for school this year. You have plenty of school clothes that fit you well enough, but that's not all there is to it. You want a whole "new look" for yourself. This year, you intend to be really special, unique in your style, all year. In fact, you would love to create a whole new style that is your own personal look. This could involve rearranging the clothes you already have or possibly adding new clothes or accessories to go with your outfits.

So far, your parents have not been too enthusiastic about all this. They have told you that you have enough clothes. They say that what you have still fits, is in good condition, and "looks very nice on you." Your present wardrobe seems quite adequate to your parents, and they like the look of your present style of dressing. You have questioned them about their opinions on styles. The new styles of today seem foolish to them. You have not been able to convince them of the value of having your own unique appearance or personal style of dressing.

What will be your goal? How will you deal with this Mess?

WE'RE MUSICAL!

Messy Situation

Do you enjoy musical plays and/or videos? Would you like to be involved in the production of a musical? Composers, artists, directors, writers and many other people all contribute to the production of a musical. Many musicals begin as the director's or writer's interpretation of a piece of music. Your challenge is to use your creative and musical skills to produce your own musical.

Plan an interpretation of a popular song or any other piece of music that you really like. You can make the interpretation in the form of a skit, video, short movie, slide show, and so forth.

Choose a popular song that does not already have a video or musical play on the market. Determine the content and mood of your selection. Plan the musical arrangement you will use, the costumes, scenery, and other things that you will need. If you need help with any of the production or actors, singers, and so on to fill the roles in your musical, you may ask others to help you.

Think about a good title, too. Consider an audience that will enjoy your performance. Present your production, if possible. How will you judge its success?

WILL IT FLY?

Messy Situation

Paper airplanes have fascinated children for years. Many and varied designs have been tried in schoolrooms (often without the permission of the teacher). Some of the designs are very good, and some aren't so good. Some fly and some flop. The secret lies in good design and careful construction and skillful paper-folding.

Build a new and better paper airplane. Do some research on flight and paper airplanes in particular. Try some different shapes and designs. Your challenge is to design the best paper airplane that you can. Make a traditional paper airplane and test it in 10 flights, measuring the distance of each flight. You must then make a new, better paper airplane that will fly at least 10 feet farther than the traditional plane's best effort!

You can use paper, paint, glue, paper clips, and so forth as part of the plane, but it should remain a paper plane. Paper should be the main material used for construction. Try to make the new airplane both attractive and aerodynamic (it must fly!). The plane must be designed to fly straight and true (it should not curve from a straight line). It should land after the flight without being damaged.

THE WINNER

Messy Situation

Congratulations!

It was recently announced that you were the winner of the grand prize in a large cash contest. Now, you can do anything that you want with the money. You have been receiving a lot of phone calls. People are stopping you in school and on the street. They all have something urgent to tell you.

All your friends (and some people who are not your friends) want you to give or loan them some money from your winnings. People want you to contribute to all kinds of different charitable causes. If you say "yes" to all the requests, you will be out of money in no time, with none left for your own wishes and dreams.

Some of the requests seem reasonable to you, and others do not. Some requests are for minor amounts of money, and some are for large amounts. Some of the requests are very appealing, especially from your closest friends. Some of the people who approach you seem to need the money desperately.

What are you going to do?

Which requests, if any, will you grant and how will you choose? How will you respond to those whose requests you are going to refuse? Make a plan for prize winners that will help them manage the money. The plan should help them to make decisions about requests and handle refusals. When your plan is complete, try to find a local prize winner or a list of the winners in a contest or lottery and send the plan to them. Ask them to write back to you about the plan and tell you if it was of any help to them.

REFERENCES

Eberle, B., & Stanish, B. (1996). *CPS for kids.* Waco, TX: Prufrock Press.

Elwell, P. (1993). *CPS for teens.* Waco, TX: Prufrock Press.

Isaksen, S. G., Dorval, K. B., & Treffinger, D. J. (2000). *Creative approaches to problem solving* (2nd ed.). Dubuque, IA: Kendall-Hunt.

Isaksen, S. G., & Treffinger, D. J. (1991). Creative learning and problem solving. In: A. Costa (Ed.), *Developing minds: A sourcebook for teaching thinking.* Alexandria, VA: Association for Supervision and Curriculum Development.

Keller-Mathers, S., & Puccio, K. (2000). *Big tools for young thinkers.* Waco, TX: Prufrock Press.

Puccio, K., Keller-Mathers, S., & Treffinger, D. (2000). *Adventures in real problem solving.* Waco, TX: Prufrock Press.

Stanish, B., & Eberle, B. (1997). *Be a problem solver.* Waco, TX: Prufrock Press.

Treffinger, D. J. (1980). *Encouraging creative learning for the gifted and talented.* Ventura, CA: Leadership Training Institute.

Treffinger, D. J. (2000a). *The creative problem solver's guidebook.* Waco, TX: Prufrock Press.

Treffinger, D. J. (2000b). *The real problem solving handbook* (2nd ed.). Waco, TX: Prufrock Press.

Treffinger, D. J., & Feldhusen, J. F. (1998). *Planning for productive thinking and learning.* Sarasota, FL: Center for Creative Learning.

Treffinger, D. J., Isaksen, S. G., & Dorval, K. B. (1994). Creative problem solving: An overview. In M. A. Runco (Ed.), *Problem finding, problem solving, and creativity.* Hillsdale, NJ: Ablex.

Treffinger, D. J., Isaksen, S. G., & Dorval, K. B. (2000). *Creative problem solving: An introduction* (3rd ed.). Waco, TX: Prufrock Press.

Treffinger, D. J., Isaksen, S. G., & Firestien, R. L. (1982). *Handbook of creative learning.* Honeoye, NY: Center for Creative Learning.

Printed in the United States
by Baker & Taylor Publisher Services